THE
GHOSTLY TALES
OF
CENTRAL
NEW YORK

Published by Arcadia Children's Books
A Division of Arcadia Publishing, Inc.
Charleston, SC
www.arcadiapublishing.com

Spooky America is a trademark of Arcadia Publishing, Inc.

First published 2024
Manufactured in the United States

Designed by Jessica Nevins
Images used courtesy of Shutterstock.com; p. 36 Mahmoud Suhail/Shutterstock.com;
p. 66 Magicpiano/File:LittleFallsNY OverlookMansion.jpg/Wikimedia Commons/CC
BY-SA 4.0.

ISBN: 978-1-4671-9761-8

Library of Congress Control Number: 2024931208

Spooky America

THE
GHOSTLY TALES
OF
CENTRAL
NEW YORK

KAREN EMILY MILLER

Adapted from Haunted Central New York by Dennis Webster

arcadia®
CHILDREN'S BOOKS

NEW YORK

PENNSYLVANIA

NEW JERSEY

VT

MA

CT

TABLE OF CONTENTS & MAP KEY

Welcome to Spooky Central New York!

Nestled between the Adirondacks and the Catskill Mountains, Central New York is home to rolling hills and farms, rivers and lakes, and beautiful waterfalls and caves—not to mention the Baseball Hall of Fame.

What a peaceful way to live! But it wasn't always that way.

This part of the country was once the ancestral home of the Iroquois peoples, but many others have tried to lay claim to the land. During the French and Indian War (1754-1763) and the American Revolutionary War (1775-1783), many battles were fought in the lands that would later become Central New York. Countless people died. It's no wonder so many ghosts roam the hills. You'll find them everywhere, from buildings near the Erie Canal to bed and breakfasts, inns, and hotels in quaint little towns.

In fact, that's what you are about to do ... on your very own ghost-hunting road trip to Central New York! Are you ready to get started?

Gerber's 1933 Tavern

Road trip! Your parents declare Central New York as the family's next travel destination. They are history buffs and want to visit the Erie Canal and battle sites of the Revolutionary War. They also love all things paranormal, and they know you do, too. So, they promise to stop at any spot with ghosts. Lucky for you, there are *a lot* of places with ghosts in this region.

You're thrilled. You've filled your backpack with all the ghost-hunting gear you've got. You have a mel meter to measure changes in electromagnetic fields, a digital camera, and even a Boo Buddy. (That's a stuffed bear set to signal if there's paranormal activity nearby.) Finally, you have a wooden flute, a gift from your parents. It's the kind said to have been used by Indigenous peoples in the area. Since Central New York is the ancestral home of the Iroquois, you might have occasion to use it. Sometimes spirits like to communicate with the living through music.

You strain to close your backpack and almost rip the zipper. You have everything you need to ghost hunt, so you're completely prepared.

Gerber's 1933 Tavern in Utica is your family's first stop. Close to the Erie Canal, the tavern was once used for seed storage. From the warehouse here, seeds were shipped all over the world. Did the seeds have anything to do with ghosts? No. It was simply a location close to the waterway that made the building a draw for spirits. Being near water is good for ghosts. There's something in the energy of moving water that helps ghosts manifest themselves. But a seed warehouse? You're going to need more convincing that this is really a ghost stop.

When you get there, you decide the tavern isn't quite as spooky looking as you'd like. You were thinking dark corners, cobwebs, and creaking doors. Instead, you find a charming place with lampshades etched with gerbera daisies. Shouldn't this place be a little spookier?

You sit down to order fried bologna sandwiches, the tavern's specialty. That's when a loaf of bread suddenly flies by your table! Startled, your dad knocks over his water glass. The server mops up the spill and says, "Did you say anything nasty about our ghosts? Sometimes they toss a loaf of bread at people who annoy them. It usually happens in the kitchen when a cook or server, who doesn't know how touchy they are, says something demeaning about spirits."

You wonder if someone at the next table criticized the ghosts. Could that be the reason for the flying bread? You look around the restaurant and see only your family there.

"Where is everyone?" asks your mom.

"The Ghost Seekers are coming to do an investigation," the server says. "Usually, people steer clear when that happens. They don't want to be in the way of an investigator and a ghost."

The Ghost Seekers? you think, impressed. You have actually heard of them. They're a professional group of paranormal investigators.

The owner stops by the table and picks up the bread loaf. "Hmm," he says. "Maybe the spirits are getting ready to greet the team."

That's when the Ghost Seekers enter the tavern. They're carrying cameras, wires, and boxes of equipment. They unpack. They have everything you have and more: digital recorders for gathering electric voice phenomenon (called EVPs for short), and K2 and Gauss meters for measuring changes in electromagnetism. One of them is carrying a hard-wired night vision camera, while another has regular digital cameras. One even has a spirit box. The spirit box searches radio frequencies and reroutes the sounds recorded into a speaker so ghost hunters can interpret them. The Ghost Seekers don't have a flute or a Boo Buddy, though.

You think it's time to make your move. You approach the leader—a lady with a nice smile. You introduce yourself and show her your flute and Boo Buddy, offering to help the Ghost Seekers in their investigation. Your parents explain the reason for the family road trip and ask if you can tag along on their hunt tonight.

Amazingly, the lady agrees. She tells you to be respectful of the ghosts. Then she asks your parents to wait outside. Too many people, she says, can spoil the investigation.

The owner turns off the lights and plunges the restaurant into darkness. He tells you it's easier to see the ghosts if it's dark. However, you forget to let your eyes adjust and stumble into a table. Feeling your way to a bar stool, you hop up and wait for instructions.

"Did you know this bar was once a speakeasy?" asks one of the team members.

You shake your head. "What's a speakeasy?"

"In the 1930s, when the government declared liquor illegal, many people looked for ways to keep drinking it. That's how speakeasies were developed. People knew that if they saw a green door in an alley, it was likely a secret entrance to a bar. They were told to "speakeasy," meaning to be quiet, as they knocked on the door. Once inside, they could dance to jazz music and drink all the alcohol they wanted.

"Can you imagine it?" the ghost hunter asks.

You give it a try. You shut your eyes and concentrate. *Hmm ...* Did you just hear the mellow tones of a clarinet? And was that a jazzy riff on a piano?

Nearby, a lady laughs out of nowhere. The sound startles you, but what you notice next sends a shiver down your spine. "Hello, suckers," the same lady says—even though you can't see her.

In an instant, you smell tobacco smoke. You hear glasses clink. You can even make out the tap of high-heeled shoes.

The laughing lady announces, "Last call!"

You open your eyes. All at once, it all disappears. There are no partygoers, no jazz band—just a dark and quiet bar. You can't help feeling amazed. You are good at imagining things, that much is true. But what if your mind *isn't* playing tricks?

The Ghost Seekers team leader leans over and whispers, "I smelled tobacco smoke."

Someone nudges you. "Are you ready to investigate?"

"Listen," says another. "*Shh . . .*"

You're so quiet you can feel the beating of your heart. Slowly, from some hidden corner, a new sound replaces your heartbeat. You hear the low hum of voices and a distant chatter. You hear something that sounds like knocking on the bar stools, almost as if the spirits are tapping time with the music.

The ghost meter springs to life with a beep.

The cameraman presses record on the digital cameras. They capture light-filled orbs scurrying back and forth in front of the screens.

There must be a ghost here somewhere.

"Please, tell us your name," a team member asks.

There's a pause.

"Harry."

You can just make out his answer, for his voice is low and hard to understand.

"Stop!" the cameraman says. "My battery is dead."

Even though he had put in fresh batteries before the investigation, something had drained all the electricity out of it. Did a ghost syphon off the energy while trying to communicate with you?

The leader asks you, "May we use your digital recorder?"

You nod, excited one of your devices will be used in a paranormal investigation.

The leader takes the team to the basement while the cameraman readies your camera and puts it on a tripod on the bar.

There's nothing in the basement. At least, nothing the devices capture.

The team gathers around the bar.

"Too bad," says one of the team. "I was certain we'd catch some paranormal activity."

You push play on your recorder. Although there is nothing you can see, you hear a hum of voices. Faint at first. It grows louder and louder until you can almost make out what the voices are saying.

Everyone smiles. The investigation has been a success. You join hands with the other seekers, and the leader asks Harry and all the other ghosts to stay.

"Don't you usually ask them to leave?" you ask.

"Not when they're having such a good time."

You think about that. You've had a good time ghost-hunting. But you don't think you'd want to spend eternity in a bar like these ghosts.

Rutger Mansion No. 3

UTICA

A tour of a famous mansion with the Ghost Seekers? You are one excited ghost hunter! The Ghost Seekers invited you to join them to investigate the famous mansions of Rutger Park, built by wealthy Uticans in the nineteenth century. Your parents agree, as long as you learn the history of each haunt.

After reading about Rutger Mansion Number 3, you discover that Samuel Morse (inventor of the Morse Code), Founding Father Alexander Hamilton, and Civil War generals all visited here. Maybe they left something of themselves in the house?

There's one historical figure who must certainly have done so. Roscoe Conkling was called a force of nature by those who knew him. He was six foot three and towered over most men. He had a booming voice that could make people cheer or shake with fear. Conkling declared himself the boss of politics in New York. No one was safe from Conkling's fury after disobeying his commands.

When the soon-to-be president of the United States, James Garfield, angered Conkling, Garfield paid for it with his life. Conkling held rallies where he declared Garfield unfit to hold political office. Conkling's angry words convinced one unstable man, Charles Guiteau, to take matters into his own hands. On July 2, 1881, Guiteau shot and killed Garfield.

No one knows if Conkling regretted what he'd said about James Garfield. He kept giving speeches. People say Conkling perfected his speaking style by practicing in front of his bedroom mirror. He'd write parts of his speeches, words he didn't want to forget, in soap on the mirror. You can't wait to check the mansion's mirrors to see if there's anything to be seen on them.

You climb the steps to the front porch and notice an owl in a nearby tree. It swivels its head to study you, almost as if checking to see if you are worthy to enter.

You shiver. You like owls, but their paranormal reputation is frightening. Some indigenous peoples believe an owl appears just before someone dies. The owl arrives to escort the soul to the next world. Others say the owl is a departing soul. You lock eyes with the owl and hope it is there for another reason—to protect the spirits that are in the house already.

As you walk through the door, a sense of heaviness hits you, making it difficult to walk. Right away, you know you're in for an exciting night.

"Please come in here," a Ghost Seeker asks, motioning to you.

You walk into a formal room and immediately experience your first ghostly encounter. A little girl, just a few years younger than you, stands by the fireplace. First, she smiles at the team member, then she turns to smile at you. She has blonde, curly hair that hangs in ringlets around her face. She's wearing an old-fashioned blue dress. Your hands tremble with fear and excitement as you fumble for the phone in your backpack. You've got to get a picture! By the time you retrieve it, though, she's gone.

The team splits up. Some go into the kitchen. The rest climb the stairs to the third floor. That's where the children's rooms are. In the nineteenth century, children weren't welcome at adult gatherings. Builders put children's rooms on the top floor and offset the staircases so the children's noise wouldn't carry downstairs.

You hope the little girl is up there.

"Turn off your flashlight," says the leader. "If there are any spirits, they'll turn on the light themselves."

With the flashlights off, the third floor is almost pitch-black. A thin ray of the setting sun filters through a window. You squint, blink, and almost gasp. A few steps away from you stands a little boy's spirit. He's there, then he's gone.

The cameraman pulls out his recorder. He says, "The last time I was here, the little boy spirit rolled a ball back and forth with me." He points the camera at the shadows and corners, hoping to get a shot.

He doesn't, but when you examine his video later, you know there was something there. The video shows glowing orbs of light.

Rustle, thud. You hear something from the corner of the room and shine your flashlight.

A child's face appears. Yikes! It flickers in and out of focus, so you can't tell if it's a boy or girl.

You're hypnotized, unable to move until you hear footsteps in the hall. The team enters the room, and the spirit child vanishes like smoke.

At first, you're disappointed. You wanted to ask the spirit some questions. But then one of the team members motions to a small door on the side of the room. *What is it?* you wonder. Could the ghost be hiding inside?

Slowly, you crack the door open. The room is no bigger than a cubby hole, but you manage to squeeze in together.

There's no sign of the ghost, but you try to speak to it anyway. "Are you a spirit?" you ask.

All of a sudden, the door slams shut, then it opens. Shut, open. Your mouth drops open, and a huge shiver darts down your spine. No gust of wind would cause the door to open and shut like that. Besides, the windows are closed. A thin whistle floats in the air, and the footsteps return to pound up and down the hallway.

A low, gruff voice mutters close by.

"Are you here?" you ask, heart racing. "Will you knock if you are?"

Moments later, a knock, heavy and firm, rattles the wall.

You grin. This is all the proof you need. You're a real ghost hunter now!

The kitchen is next on your list. The team gathers around the kitchen table and waits. But not for long. The temperature drops ten degrees in five minutes.

Something is here with us, you think. Is it one of the same ghost children? Or ... has another spirit entered the room?

Out of the corner of your eye, you see movement in the pantry.

"Oh!" exclaims one of the team members. She sits straight up in her chair, poised almost as if she's ready to run. "I can see her inside my head," the team member says. "A middle-aged woman with black hair tied up in a bun. Oh, no!" she pauses for a moment. "She looks angry."

"I sense the letter 'R', another member adds.

The team's medium (that's a person who

claims to have special, paranormal abilities that allow them to communicate with spirits) closes his eyes and concentrates. "I think her name is Ruth. She's annoyed because even though she's the head of the kitchen staff, she has to run back and forth from the kitchen to the dining room." He chuckles. "Maybe one of the serving maids is sick?"

You'd be irritated, too, if you had to run back and forth between rooms for all eternity.

"I saved the best for last," says the leader. "It's the library."

You follow the Ghost Seekers into the library

and look around. The library must have once been beautiful. Chandeliers give the room a glow. The wallpaper is unlike any you've seen, detailed with scenes from around the world. One of the scenes shows a snake curling up at the base of a palm tree. You can imagine how colorful the walls looked when the wallpaper was first hung.

"Look at the fireplace," someone whispers.

You turn and see something coiling and uncoiling in front of the fireplace. It's an ectoplasm, you realize excitedly: a glowing, green, slippery-looking blob that floats in the air, shifting shapes, stretching from a basketball shape to that of a sticky-looking surfboard. It's more gross than terrifying.

At the same time you spot it, a knock sounds, and a faint female voice calls—it's your team member in the distance.

The ectoplasm curls its way toward you. You don't want to walk through it to get to the door. You wait for it to disappear before you leave to join the team.

You meet up with the group to discuss what you've seen. You didn't see any words on Conkling's mirror, but you've had plenty of excitement.

As you all collapse into chairs, you hear a low and menacing growl. You don't know what it is, but it sounds like it wants you gone.

"Are you happy we're here?" the leader asks, trying to address the ghostly presence.

Another growl. Then, an

answer you don't like to hear. "*No!*" The voice is gruff and angry.

Who is it? you wonder. Could it be Ruth? The little boy? The little girl? Or maybe even . . . *Conkling* himself?

"*GO!*" commands the spirit.

You decide that the angry voice has to belong to Conkling. You don't have to be told twice.

You jump up and exit quickly, along with the rest of the team.

Once outside, your team exchanges high fives. The Rutger No. 3 mansion had more ghosts than you could have imagined.

"Do you want to go on another investigation?" the leader asks.

You think for a minute. Nothing has pushed or shoved you. You have been startled and surprised. But have you been scared? Not really. Not yet. After all, you came to Central New York *looking* for a ghost challenge! You're not backing down now.

"I'm ready," you answer.

The Stanley Theater

The Stanley Theater

Utica

"It's cold with a full moon...perfect for a haunting." That's what your mom says as she drops you off at the Stanley Theater, one of Utica's most visited landmarks.

You wave goodbye and walk into the Stanley. Your dad told you that it was originally called a "movie palace," and the lobby does look like the inside of a castle. There are gold-leaf columns, towering ceilings, and a grand staircase with ornate gold railings.

Your mom told you that the Stanley Theater differed from most American theaters. "Mexican Baroque," she called it, referring to the theater's style and design. All the walls, ceilings, and floors are covered with gold gilt and swirling designs. Heavy curtains line the stage.

You'd stop to admire it, but you have a special place you want to see ... the ghost row on the balcony! Years before, when men greased back their hair with oil, their heads would leave a mark on the wall behind them.

In dim light, the greasy spots on the wall made it look like the row was filled with shadow people. Some say it looked like a line of ghosts.

When you get up to the balcony, you realize the back wall is now covered by a plexiglass shield. You find out that the owners of the Stanley Theater added the shield after the building's last renovation. You're sorry they improved it. You could squint all you liked, but you wouldn't see the smeared headprints that looked like ghostly heads.

But you're not discouraged. You know there are plenty of ghosts to be found inside this spooky theater. After many trips back and

forth to the van to get equipment, including tape-down wires for the cameras, you're ready to hunt.

The team assigns you to the ladies' bathroom on the ground floor of the theater. You're happy when several of the Ghost

Seekers say they'll come with you. You want to see some more ghosts, but you'd rather not be alone. Especially if you run into any ladies who don't want you in there!

When you enter the bathroom and take a seat on the tile floor, the ghost hunter begins talking in a very quiet voice.

"Please excuse us for invading your space," she

says. "Will you click on the flashlight if you're here with us?"

Immediately, the flashlight flickers on.

Maybe it's the cold tile floor beneath you, or maybe it's a ghost—either way, a shiver runs right up your spine! You almost grab the team member sitting next to you but hesitate. What if you grab the ghost instead? You hold yourself tightly and shudder. You're having a great time—and the spookiness is just getting started!

Before long, you feel a blanket of cold come over you. It's like sitting in fog. This, though, isn't the pearly gray curtain that rolls off a lake. *This* fog is a cloud of inky black that feels like it's covering you in slime as it sweeps over your body.

The team leader whispers, "Got your Boo Buddy?"

Proudly, you pull out the stuffed bear and turn it on. Then you place it on the floor in front of you.

Right away, your Boo Buddy speaks! "Brr . . . it's cold in here."

"I haven't heard that before," a team member says. "The bear is sensing changes in the electromagnetic force field or temperature. It also talks if someone or something touches it."

The bear giggles. "Tee hee. That tickles."

You are shocked. Besides you, no one has touched the bear!

"Tee hee. That tickles."

"The spirit likes your bear," says the cameraperson.

Another member says, "I saw a ghostly girl named Mary in a dream last night. Mary, is that you with us?"

This time Boo Buddy is quiet. You all hear a disembodied voice that sounds like it is coming from around twenty feet away. It's accompanied by a whimpering sound, like someone is about to burst into tears.

"May I move closer to you?" the team leader asks.

"No!" says a voice suddenly. After a time, it begins to whimper again.

That's when you all start to notice a column of black smoke rising in the far corner of the bathroom.

The cameramen turn on their recorders.

The smoke flickers and sways, almost as if it's about to reveal something. But as hard

as you try, you can't see anything but smoke. Eventually, the smoke fades away like it was never there at all.

Phew, you think. All that paranormal activity on your first stop! You hope this is only the beginning.

Your group heads to the belly of the theater next—a tunnel under the seats! You learn that the tunnel was used to spirit actors from one location to another so they could make surprise appearances during plays. Perhaps now the theater's ghosts use it for their *own* surprise appearances?

When you were small, tunnels scared you. They were, in your opinion, dark and musty. Who knew what kinds of scary things awaited you in the shadows? Now, you're ready for whatever is there. You're older now and you're with professional ghost hunters.

You head into the tunnel with your eyes and ears on high alert. It's quiet—so still that all you hear is the slight hum of electric panels. You take a few steps then stop. A shadow has darted past you. Your nose detects a gust of perfume, heavy and smelling of decayed fruit. Then, a cloud of cold settles all around you. You shiver, wishing you'd brought your jacket.

"It's almost 11:30 p.m.," says the leader. "We'll have to hurry."

The team climbs the stairs to the mezzanine, the balcony block of seats that hangs over the main floor.

"People say there's a . . . "

"A man," you whisper with a gasp. "I see a *man!*"

About thirty feet away stands a tall, skinny shadow man with a wide-brimmed hat. The outline reminds you of a farmer.

Before you can ask him if he's a ghost, he dissolves through a wall. He leaves nothing behind but a heartbreaking moan.

"A séance," suggests a team member. "That's what we must do."

You know all about séances, special gatherings where you try to contact the spirit world. You've had them before with friends at sleepovers.

You all sit in a circle around a table in the lobby. Digital recorders, hand-held ghost detectors, and a candle are set on the table's surface.

You all close your eyes and hold hands,

concentrating hard. Soon, the spirits are ready for you. The team leader says he feels a cold breath on his neck. Then something scratches his arm. Another ghost hunter feels a blazing heat *inside* his left arm and a bone-chilling cold in his right.

Your leader says, "Something is sending electrical currents through my hands."

"The ghosts must be trying to use our energy to make themselves known," says another.

A moment later, he asks, "What's that?"

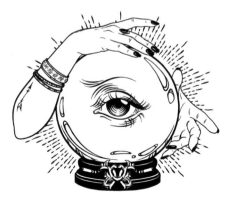

Standing behind one of the ghost hunters is a *singing* shadow. Is this another spirit? Trapped to sing in the Stanley Theater forever?

The ghost meter spikes. The camera's batteries go dead.

Everyone agrees that it's a sign to end the ghost hunt. You've gotten plenty of ghostly evidence—more than you had hoped for. Still, you're sorry to go. The Stanley Theater gave you a paranormal performance better than any movie you've seen.

CHAPTER 4

Shoppes at the Finish Line

UTICA

It's 7:00 p.m.— time for some more haunting! You never expected to be sitting in a pub with pinball machines and blaring TVs. Still, you like all the spooky souvenirs for sale: hats, shirts, even coffee mugs. With all the merchandise advertising ghosts, something has *got* to be paranormal in the Shoppes at the Finish Line.

Your parents told you that an underground river explains the paranormal activity here.

The Shoppes were once the site of a woolen mill, where big spinning machines spun animal fiber into fabric. Mills need water to turn their wheels, so the building was built directly above a creek fed by an underground river. Ghost hunters know spirits use water as extra energy to make themselves known to the living.

Over 150 years old, the three-story red brick building definitely looks old enough to host some ghosts.

You've checked and rechecked your backpack. A team investigator smiles when you show him your gear.

"This place is so haunted, we might need more equipment," he says. Suddenly, he pushes back his chair and stands up. "Hear that?"

You do hear something. It's the scraping sound furniture makes when it's moved across the floor. The question is, who could be moving it?

"Let's go," you say.

You're wiping away sweat by the time you reach the third floor. Maybe you didn't need to pack two digital recorders. But you wanted an extra. Having no or little energy of their own, the spirits suck energy from wherever they can. You want to be ready in case that happens.

At first, the third floor looks disappointing.

It's a storage room and holds shelves and shelves of boxes. You see plenty of old furniture, but no ghosts. At least . . . not *yet.*

The team leader turns off the lights, explaining that ghosts don't seem to like them. You stand still to let your eyes adjust to the dark. You don't want to bump into a ghost. Then you pull out a recorder and press "record."

All is silent . . . until it isn't. Out of nowhere, heavy footsteps thud behind you—making you jump. A moan curls out of a corner. You're glad you are recording this. Otherwise, would anyone believe you?

It's so dusty up here that you begin to sneeze.

Maybe that's why you miss seeing the shadow man skitter across the room. You must have shut your eyes while you sneezed!

"Don't be disappointed," the team leader says. "You'll see ghosts tonight. We have two more floors to investigate."

You hope she's right.

However, when you go down to the second floor, you doubt it. It seems an unlikely place for ghosts. It's full of furniture and gift shops. Then, suddenly, there's a tap on your shoulder. You look to where the leader is pointing.

Thanks to his flashlight, you spot an old woman shuffling among the shadows across the room. You can tell she's old because she moves in short, tentative steps, almost as if it hurts her to walk. You look more closely at her. She certainly doesn't look like the grandmothers you've seen in storybooks. She doesn't smile or have shiny white hair. She certainly doesn't hold out a plate of cookies.

Instead, she looks like a hag, or even a storybook witch. Inky, oily black hair reaches down to her waist. She raises her hands and wiggles crooked fingers in the air. She stretches out her arms toward you, and you back away, swallowing hard. *She can't want a hug, can she?*

You almost trip over the camera cable taped to the floor as you move away. From a safe distance, you gather enough courage to ask the spirit, "Why are you here?"

The hag shakes her head and backs away into the dark. Then, just as quickly as she appeared, she's gone.

Before you can worry too much about where the ghostly woman went, a high-pitched cry that sounds like it's coming from a small child arises in another corner. Right away, you hear the team leader's digital recorder click on.

"It's the boy spirit—the one other ghost teams have mentioned," the team medium explains. "They say his name is Nicholas."

Nicholas, you think, concentrating as hard as you can. *Can you hear us?*

"Are you a little boy?" the medium asks. "If so, please turn on the flashlight."

The light turns on.

"If your name is Nicholas, will you please switch off the flashlight?"

The flashlight goes dark.

By this time, the rest of the team has joined you.

"It's active here," says the team leader. "The ghost meters are spiking. Let's sit around the table and see what else happens."

You've just sat down when a shadow person materializes directly behind the cameraman. A phantom chin digs into your right shoulder. "Ouch!"

The cameraman slumps and almost drops his camera. "I can feel my energy being sucked away!"

You don't think little Nicholas would attack any of you. Who could it be?

"Remember the story about Conrad Hahl?" the team leader asks. You do.

"Over a hundred years ago, when the building housed a mill, workers had to be careful. A mill can be dangerous. But the mill machinery didn't hurt him. It was the elevator.

While fixing it, he got his leg stuck in the elevator door.

No one knows if someone pushed the elevator button.

When the elevator began rising, so did Conrad Hahl's leg. By the time the elevator stopped, his foot and part of his leg had been ripped off. The doctors amputated the rest of Conrad's leg, hoping to stop the spreading gangrene, a condition that causes human tissue to turn purple, green, and black before it dies. But days later, Conrad passed away.

Was Conrad angry? You would be, you tell yourself. What a terrible way to die.

The others say Conrad Hahl is a nasty spirit. No one likes him, not even the other ghosts. If Conrad's paying a visit, the other ghosts will not.

You gather your courage to speak. You don't want to anger him. "Were you killed in an elevator accident?"

Thump. The floor almost rattles with its force. The another knock follows, equally powerful. A growl, low and menacing, fills the room.

The leader says it's time to move. Maybe she notices a few of you are trembling.

You return to the bar. The TVs are off. The pinball machines are still. It's quiet and dark. An investigator lights a candle to draw the spirits, and you gather around to join hands.

The team leader nods to you. She's giving you another chance to communicate with the spirits.

"Are you Conrad Hahl?"

A shadow moves across the table, then evaporates.

"Are you the old lady who lives upstairs?" the medium asks. He says he thinks she's also in the room.

The candle sputters. Its flame shoots up and down several times. It wavers back and forth, almost as if someone is trying to blow it out.

You think that Conrad Hahl and the hag are here.

"Why are so grumpy, Conrad?" asks the medium. "You scare Nicholas when you act this way."

He doesn't get a response.

"I think you're nothing but a control freak," the medium adds.

Uh oh, you think. There's going to be trouble now.

You're right. Suddenly, something pushes a team member's chair away from the table. It's done with such force that you're surprised he doesn't fall on the floor. Somehow, though, he manages to keep upright, his hands joined in the circle.

"Nicholas is hiding," the cameraman says. "We need to find a way to draw him to us."

"I have the Boo Buddy in my backpack," you say. You hope it works. It's your bear's time to shine, or at least, to flicker.

The cameraman puts your Boo Buddy on the table alongside a flashlight and ghost meters.

You say, "Nicholas, would you like to touch the bear?"

Everything reacts. The meters buzz and chime. Something must have touched the bear's paw because its light flashes.

The team leader asks, "Are you happy in the afterlife? If you are, would you please turn on the flashlight."

Not only does the flashlight click on, it rolls off the table into the leader's lap! A ghostly orb appears and circles the Boo Buddy for a moment or two. Then it disappears.

You disappear, too, right after you pack up your gear.

What a night! Two ghosts who won't leave because their anger keeps them stuck. Maybe it's a good idea for them to stay inside the

Shoppes. No one would want them wandering the streets of Utica. Nicholas, though, makes you think. Why hasn't he left the Shoppes? You don't know why he's stuck in the building. However, after tonight's session, you're certain he is happy where he is. That makes you happy, too.

The Overlook Mansion

The Overlook Mansion

Little Falls

Can sadness hold a ghost in place? You're about to find out at the Overlook Mansion. About fifty years ago, a family lived there. Four of the children had been adopted from their home on the Crow Nation Reservation in Montana. People thought the children would be happy. Their adoptive parents were wealthy, and their new home, the Overlook Mansion, was like a castle.

Still, rumors said the children were miserable. Two of the brothers were so unhappy that they ran away. Perhaps they planned to return to their home in Montana and the family they had left behind. Maybe they thought jumping a train would get them back there.

The boys made it to the railroad tracks. But they never made it onto the train. Perhaps they tried to jump into an open train car and fell. When the search party found them, their bodies were next to the tracks.

Did their spirits find their way back to the Overlook Mansion? Or are other unhappy ghosts residing there? You hope you'll find out tonight. You've been invited to investigate Overlook Mansion with the Ghost Seekers. No family lives there now. Instead, it's a bed and breakfast—a small inn.

The team is here at the request of the mansion's caretaker. Even though he sleeps on the second floor, he says he hears noises from the kitchen most nights. Low voices, rattling dishes, and sounds that shouldn't carry are loud enough to wake him from a deep sleep. He says he races down the stairs and flings open the kitchen door, hoping to catch the trespasser— but always, the kitchen is empty. The caretaker has accustomed himself to the noises, but guests have been frightened. Several said they had felt a scary presence in their rooms.

They might not have enjoyed their stays, but you are sure you will.

The Overlook Mansion sits atop a hillside above the town of Little Falls. The team follows the driveway's curves up a steep hill. You're glad your investigation isn't taking place during a storm. You'd hate to slide off the road.

The team parks in front of the mansion. With its bright red roof and gray stone, it looks more like a castle than a house. Three turrets and twenty-six rooms ... lots of places to explore.

You stop on the landing to admire the stained-glass window. Light streams through it. It's hypnotizing. Admiring the colored lights, you almost miss your first ghost. A shadow person materializes on the second floor. Its outline is vague—almost transparent—so you can't tell if it's an adult or child, man or woman. By the time you get to the second

floor, it's gone. However, you hear footsteps tripping down the hall away from you.

Downstairs in the lobby, another team member has his own ghostly encounter. He is jotting notes about the house when, suddenly, a book flies off a shelf and slams into his chest! He bends over and picks up the book. A book of prayers.

How could it have flown off the shelf with such force? The answer seems clear: a ghost, of course! Two team members prepare for a walk-through in the basement. Walk-throughs are standard operating procedure. Before you set up cameras, you have to determine where there is paranormal activity.

When the team assembles, you smell the rotten egg stench of sulfur. Two ghost hunters join you and report they felt faint while walking through the kitchen. The medium senses a child's spirit in the dining room.

Ghosts above, ghosts below. There are spirits everywhere at the Overlook!

Where should you start? You choose the basement for obvious reasons. For one thing, basements are known to be creepy, and sometimes downright terrifying. (So, what better place to look for ghosts?) For another, investigators often connect with the paranormal in underground spaces. The team members who checked it out earlier said there were signs of paranormal activity down there. You're so excited you almost trip coming down the stairs. You tell yourself that it's not because you're afraid; it's because you're balancing a camera in one hand and a mel meter in the other. The mel meter measures changes in the electromagnetic field, or EMF. Spirits cause a shift in the EMF, and the meter measures it. Both the camera and the mel meter are fragile, and you don't want to drop either of them.

By the time you make it to the basement, you see the others who got there before you pointing to a spot in a corner. There's movement—more of a scurry—as a shadow person retreats deeper into the dark.

Maybe that spirit doesn't want to communicate with you, but other entities aren't so shy. You ask questions using the "knock-knock" method. That's where one or two knocks can give a "Yes" or "No" answer to a question. You concentrate to make sure you hear the knocks correctly. In fact, you're concentrating so hard you don't even notice when something—or someone—faintly touches your arm. After a minute or two, you become aware of the pressure. Your heartbeat picks up. Who ... or *what* ... is squeezing your arm? When you finally build up the courage to look down, there's nothing there.

You're glad to go to your next stop, the dining room, where you hear footsteps followed by a ghostly voice. It's high-pitched, so you guess it comes from a child's spirit.

It's time for your surprise investigation tool, your cedarwood flute.

You knew it might come in handy, and you're glad you brought it.

You play a few notes, wishing you knew songs from the Crow people. You also wish

you had practiced more because your first flute notes come out like squeaks. Finally, you manage a few true notes.

The handheld ghost devices light up, and a strong perfume settles over you. Before you can investigate further, you hear an excited voice from the kitchen. It's a human voice—the team leader.

She says, "I believe we've found a portal to the other side. You've got to come in here."

As soon as you enter, you spot another shadow person pop up, then instantly vanish. Then something pushes you so hard that you bump into the kitchen table.

Something yells, "Huff!" It sounds like a "Boo!" in a scary movie. It scares you and you rush off for the second floor.

Faint voices echo from a bedroom. Orbs of all sizes circle the room. Once inside, knocks and more huffs follow. This time, you aren't startled, and you stay to examine the bedroom. It had belonged to one of the family's daughters. She had suffered from tuberculosis, a disease that affects the lungs. She spent a lot of time on the balcony outside the room. At that time, people thought fresh air might cure the disease.

As you stand on the balcony, you feel, then *see*, a spirit. It's too quick for you to study it, but it's there all the same.

One of the team asks if the spirit is the

sickly daughter. The orbs have disappeared, along with the knocks, but the bed begins to shake. It vibrates just like the ones in motels of long ago, where you put in a coin and let the jiggling mattress relax you.

A chill runs up your spine

when a ghostly child appears suddenly and looks at you. It's almost as if *you* all are the paranormal beings, and she is the ghost hunter examining you! Before you can study her carefully, she disappears into the closet door. Your flashlights, which are still in your pockets, flash on and off.

What a night! Later, you watch the camera feed from the ghost hunt. You're glad you didn't see all that was there when you investigated. It turns out there was so much paranormal activity, you wouldn't have known what to investigate and what to ignore! Orbs and spirit lights floated around you. On the second floor, the camera recorded a ghostly face staring at you through a window. No human could have done that. The window was thirty feet off the ground.

The video shows a face flickering in a dining

room mirror. In the basement, a large smudge of inky ectoplasm floats in front of the camera.

"I'm drained," says a team member.

Even though teachers at school have said you have the energy to spare, you don't now. You feel exhausted, too. All that paranormal activity sapped everyone. It's time to go.

Later, when you help pack up the gear, you look at your watch. Only a few hours have

passed. All that spooky activity in just a few hours!

You smile to yourself. What a carnival ride this night had been. And just like a popular ride, it was worth the wait.

Orchard Hall

SAUQUOIT

Orchard Hall doesn't look like a speakeasy. There's no secret door on the side, and it's not hidden in a dark alley. Warm amber light shines through the etched-glass front doors and lights up the column-lined portico. It looks like a nineteenth-century mansion, exactly what it was before the Prohibition era of the 1930s.

That's when the government outlawed alcohol sales. Orchard Hall became one of the few places in Sauquoit where you could secretly buy liquor. You can imagine angry voices outside the mansion, men pounding on the front door and yelling, "Open up! It's the law!"

You picture the speakeasy boss at the window, balancing clanking boxes of liquor bottles as he lowers them from the second story. His men race into the nearby apple orchard to hide the liquor. When the police leave, the bottles return to shelves in the secret bar.

"The owner must have made a lot of money," you say. "It looks like a rich person lives here."

"It's not a speakeasy anymore," says the Ghost Seekers' cameraman. "It's a restaurant, and the owners work hard. The ghosts, though, have it easy. All they have to do is haunt."

Ghosts often haunt the place where they

experienced trauma in life. Julia Butler, the most famous resident ghost at Orchard Hall, is said to have died in the Red Room, a bedroom upstairs. Some say she may have lived here long ago and died during childbirth. That explains, people say, why the rocking chair in the Red Room moves by itself. "It's Julia rocking her baby," the restaurant owners explain.

Others say Julia didn't die in childbirth. They think Julia was shot in the bar, then died from her wounds upstairs.

When you're assigned to investigate the Red Room, you're super excited. You can't help it. It should be the most haunted room in the house.

You unpack your equipment and sit on the bed to wait

for any sign of Julia's presence. Even though you look at your ghost meter multiple times, the needle stays put.

Hmm.

Where is Julia Butler? The owners tell you there have been many hauntings in the past. In the 1970s, locals booked weddings at Orchard House because of its beautiful setting. The bridal parties looked elegant posing on the front staircase.

One photographer got a surprise when he developed the wedding pictures. Standing next to the bride stood a ghostly white figure. What convincing proof that a spirit lived here! Sadly, the picture disappeared a few years later, but many people said they remembered it and swore there was a ghost in the photo.

One of the team members tells you about the piano player and singer. The couple often entertained at the Orchard House. One night, their music brought out more than the usual fans. It's said that Julia appeared, too.

The entertainers finished their performance and packed up their equipment, ready to go home to Lake George. However, during the evening, a winter storm had blown in. The roads were impassable.

The owners worried about the couple's safety. "Stay in one of our bedrooms," they said.

So, the couple did, along with their two dogs.

It seemed like a good idea.

The two settled down in bed with their dogs at their feet. They were almost asleep when they heard footsteps.

Thump! Thump! The footsteps, faint at first, grew louder and louder until they sounded like they were just outside their door.

Slowly, almost painfully so, the bedroom door creaked open. Then it slammed shut.

According to the couple, the dogs ran to the door. They barked and growled until the wife flung open the door. No one was there.

Had the dogs been protecting the couple from something? They didn't stay to find out. They threw their clothes into their suitcases,

packed up the dogs, and left.

Most people wouldn't return. The couple did. They were professionals and had promised to perform the next week. When they returned to Orchard Hall this time, they weren't frightened. They were robbed!

The wife's datebook of scheduled shows went missing.

The owners said that perhaps the ghost was only borrowing the datebook. And indeed, the very next week, it showed up next to the microphone stand! (Maybe the ghost wanted to be sure not to miss any of the couple's upcoming performances?)

Remembering those stories, you decide not to give up. There's a ghost here, somewhere.

You decide to try your luck in another part of Orchard Hall. You get up from the bed, turn off the Red Room's lights, and close the door behind you. Then, remembering you left your ghost meter on the bed, you go back to the room. To your surprise, the lights are on! A shiver darts through you. You're *certain* you turned them off.

After grabbing the ghost meter, you turn off the lights again. You double-check that every light is off. They are. The room is in total darkness. You step outside, close the door, and wait.

A few moments later, a ray of light escapes from under the door. But before you can investigate, you hear screams coming from the restaurant.

You pound down the stairs and run to the bar. There, two ladies are pointing to the ceiling. A piece of the ceiling light has fallen on the bar, narrowly missing the women.

"What happened?" you ask.

The owner shrugs his shoulders and says, "They were making fun of our ghosts."

Ah, you say to yourself. Maybe the ladies woke up the spirits. Sometimes spirits need to be prodded before they make an appearance. You run back up to the Red Room. This time, your ghost meters spike and chime. The rocking chair stays still. However, you're convinced there's going to be more paranormal activity.

When you rejoin the team, they are standing outside the ladies' bathroom on the first floor.

"A woman just ran out," the cameraman says. "She said there was a lady who jumped into the bathroom stall and tried to grab her. All she remembers is that she wore black velvet gloves."

You start to open the bathroom door, but the owner stops you. "Don't go in there."

The team leader goes in instead. You can hear her ghost meters chime and buzz.

"I want you to see something." The owner leads you into a side room. Hanging on the walls are pictures of Orchard Hall through the years. One of them looks different from the others. Instead of the inscription, *Orchard Hall, 1842*, the house has a different name.

"Butler Hall," the inscription reads.

As in ... Julia Butler.

You smile. So, Julia did live here after all.
Is that why she refuses to leave Orchard Hall?
Some spirits just never want to leave home.

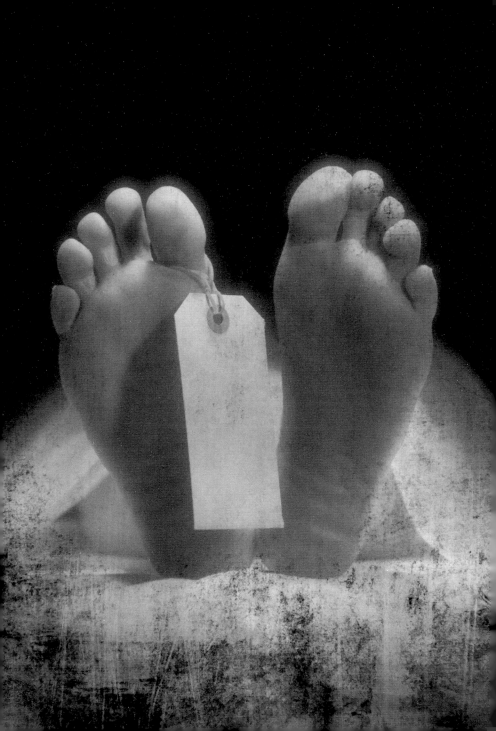

Suiter Mansion

HERKIMER

You know houses can be haunted. Churches? *Yes*. Graveyards? *Certainly*. But what about . . . a table? The ghost-hunting team is headed to Herkimer, New York, to find out.

As you pull up to the Suiter Mansion, you once again doubt the team's choice of haunts. What's so spooky about this house? Built by a local doctor, it was used as his office, waiting room, and personal library. But he never lived there.

No one lives there now. The local historical society uses it to house artifacts and documents from the past.

There are two mahogany doors at the top of the house steps. Carved into the wood you see two mythological griffins, creatures with lion's bodies and bird's heads. They look so real you think the bird's eyes track you as you knock on the door.

Inside, there's an intricately carved staircase in the front hall. In the library, there's a tiled fireplace with pictures of Greek gods and goddesses. It's hard to believe something paranormal is here. It's too beautiful. Half of the Ghost Seekers examine the attic, and the other half, the basement. You make sure you're on the team that's going to the attic. That's where the haunted table is stored.

When you reach the attic, you're a little confused. The table looks ... ordinary. You could imagine yourself sitting at it, eating a bowl of cereal. It's just a flat wooden rectangle held up by six support legs. There are no curves, no carvings. It's nothing like the rest of the house.

That is, until the medium explains what makes this table different from the one in your kitchen at home.

"It's an *autopsy* table," he says.

Your eyes grow wide. An autopsy table is where a pathologist, a specially trained doctor, cuts open bodies to see how and why someone died. Nowadays, autopsies are usually performed in hospitals. In the late nineteenth century, though, autopsies were often done in a doctor's home, where many doctors saw their patients.

When performing an autopsy, a doctor examines the corpse inside and out. Sometimes, they remove internal organs for tests. They also collect samples of tissue and bodily fluids. It's a messy business. The fluids and tissues find their way into the cracks and fissures of the wood.

Scrubbing can't remove it all. Each time, some of that person remains behind in the table.

Dr. Suiter was a pathologist, you find out, and a very good one. That's why the county sent him murder cases—and why the spirits are so restless here. Many of them died in trauma.

After learning all this, the table suddenly looks more menacing to you. You wonder, how many spirits remain trapped inside the wood? What terrifying stories would this table tell, if it could talk?

You can't stay in the attic for very long because you have been assigned a turn at Ghost Central: that's what the Ghost Seekers call a ghost-free spot in the house, where a large screen can be setup to show the camera feeds. Earlier, some of the team checked to make sure there weren't any presences nearby. A spirit might disrupt a session.

As you pull up your chair next to the other Ghost Central member, you think about that autopsy table with its trapped spirits. For once, you're happy to be in a ghost-free zone.

Your fellow ghost hunter is grateful for your help at Ghost Central. "We have six feeds showing up on the screen. It's hard for one person to catch everything."

You sit up in your chair, feeling important. You promise yourself that nothing will get past you. If there's a ghost, you'll spot it.

One team goes to the attic, the other to the basement. No question was asked, not one meter engaged, before ghostly orbs appeared in all the feeds. This would be a special investigation!

You study the camera feed from the attic. The room is filled with boxes from the historical society. And, of course, there's the table.

Our medium puts his hands on the table. "My body's lighting up with energy from the other side!" Slowly, he pulls away his hands. "There's a female presence on the table."

Another Ghost Seeker races to the table and puts her hands on it. "It's as hot as a stovetop!" She jumps back from the table.

Everyone lays their ghost meters on the table, along with their flashlights.

"Dr. Suiter, are you here?"

The flashlight clicks on. The ghost meters chime on and off.

Is the spirit of Dr. Suiter signaling us?

Suddenly, orbs fill the room, whirling and dancing above our heads.

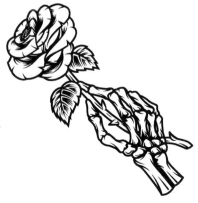

"Will you please knock if you're a ghost?"

Two hard knocks follow.

The medium lays his hands on the table once more. "I sense a female presence." He closes his eyes. "Her name is Rebecca." He asks the spirit to turn on the flashlight if he is correct.

Not only does the flashlight beam, the K2 meter spikes!

Later, the attic team joins the others in the basement. That's where Dr. Suiter stored the

cadavers before he autopsied them. And that's when chaos breaks out. Footsteps pound across the floor. The feed from the camera shakes and quivers, even though no one is touching it. After a few moments of this, the team leader shakes her head and says, "I've had enough."

Everyone agrees they have enough evidence for their investigation.

You volunteer to help retrieve gear from the basement. You feel strong and ready to help. After all, you haven't had your energy sapped by the ghosts like the others.

You're standing at the top of the stairs, holding the last recorder, when you hear a voice behind you. It's sweet and clear—a woman's voice. You can't understand her words, but you sense they are pleasant. Your mind and body fill with a happy, peaceful sensation. You can't explain it, but something tells you without a doubt that it's Rebecca, the ghost. It has to be.

"Too bad we turned off the recorders," says the cameraman. "No one will hear this."

You aren't too upset. Your visit to Central New York has given you enough proof of the paranormal to last a lifetime. It was a nice way

to end a ghost hunt. Rebecca's ghost sent you off with friendly words, not threats and growls. After all, when you're seeking the spirits, what more can you really ask for?

A Ghostly Goodbye

You've had a ghost-filled tour of Central New York. You've met nice ghosts, like the lady Rebecca at Dr. Suiter's house, and scary ones, like Roscoe Conkling at the Utica Mansion. Along with spotting ghosts, you've eaten fried bologna sandwiches and sampled special sausage hot dogs. When you weren't out ghost hunting, you visited the Baseball Hall of Fame and Revolutionary War sites and saw waterfalls and caves. No wonder so many people and ghosts have come to visit, and many, to stay.

Some say it's because the region has so many lakes, streams, ponds, and swamps for ghosts to use as energy sources. Perhaps the rolling hills, forests, and farmland of Central New York brought them here. Whatever it was, they've chosen to stay forever. You decide to come back soon. There are many more you have yet to see!

KAREN EMILY MILLER has been writing about strange creatures since she was six years old, so writing about the paranormal is a perfect fit. She just moved to Iowa City and is excited to meet new ghosts there.

Check out some of the other *Spooky America* titles available now!

Spooky America was adapted from the creeptastic *Haunted America* series for adults. *Haunted America* explores historical haunts in cities and regions across America. Here's more from the original *Haunted Central New York* author, Dennis Webster: